Reading

K
Kindergarten

▶ Trace.

 cat

 hat

 van

 mat

▶ Connect the dots. What is it?

B ●   ● C

A ━━━━━━━━ 🌸 D   ● E

● G   ● F

_____ on a _____

▶ Trace.

 r e d

 t e n

 b e d

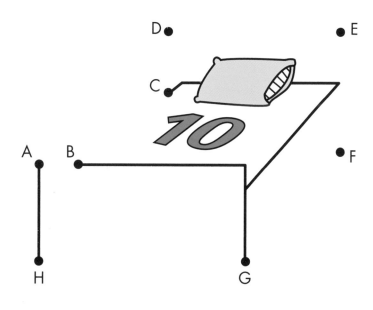 p e n

▶ Connect the dots. What is it?

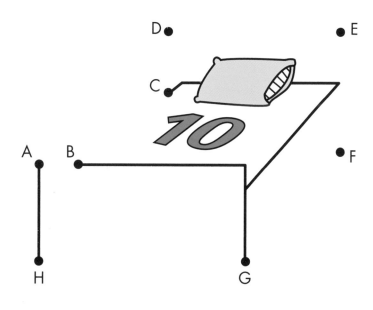

D ●   ● E

C ●

A ● B ●   ● F

H   G

_____ _____ on a _____

▶ Trace.

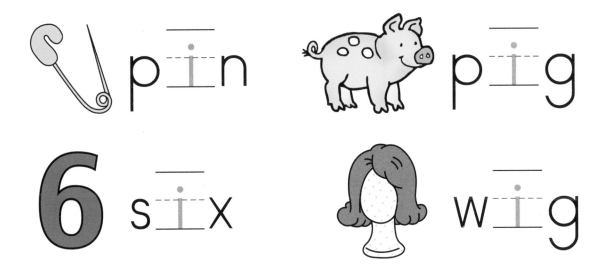

pin   pig

6 six   wig

▶ Connect the dots. What is it?

B
C
A
6
D
P
N Q
O
E H
I J M
G
F K L

_____   _____

on a _____

▶ Trace.

f o x   m o p

b o x   p o t

▶ Connect the dots. What is it?

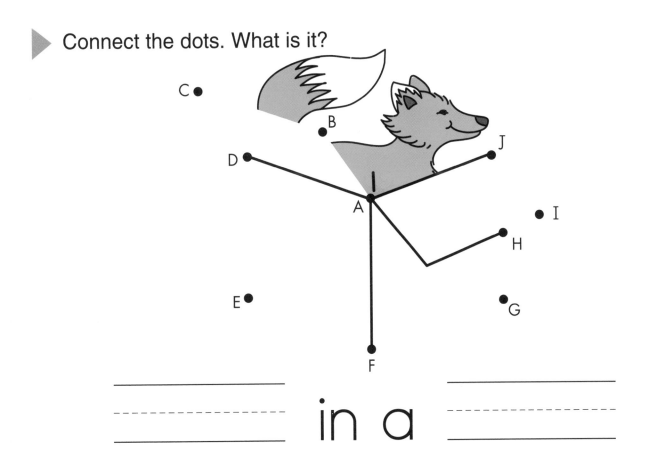

_____ in a _____

▶ Trace.

r u g   s u n

b u s   b u g

▶ Connect the dots. What is it?

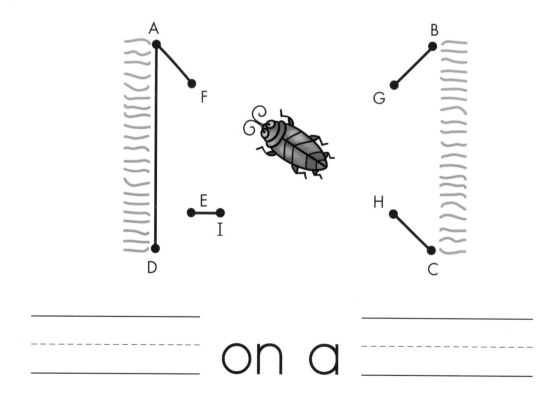

_____   _____

on a _____

EMC 4178 • © Evan-Moor Corp.

red box

pig in mud

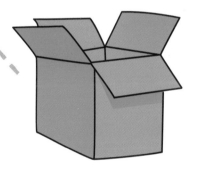

mop in the sun

cat on a rug

▶ **Read the story.**

The cat sat on the hat.
The hat is flat.
Bad cat!
Run, cat, run!

▶ **Read. Draw.**

I can fix the hat.

EMC 4178 • © Evan-Moor Corp.

▶ Trace.

h a̅ nd   l a̅ mp

s a̅ nd   m a̅ sk

▶ Connect the dots. What is it?

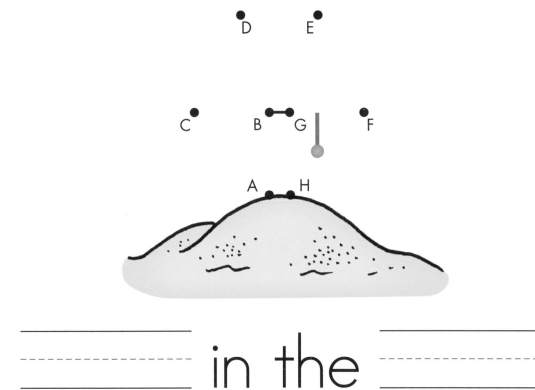

_____ in the _____

Trace.

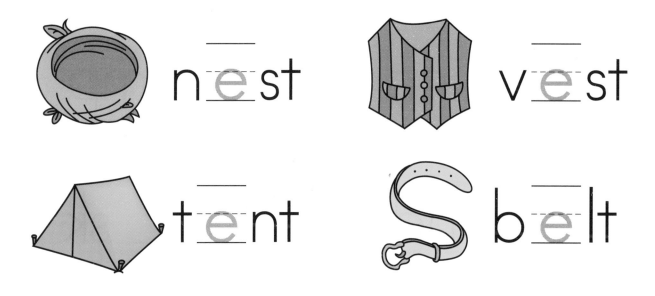

n e s t

v e s t

t e n t

S b e l t

Connect the dots. What is it?

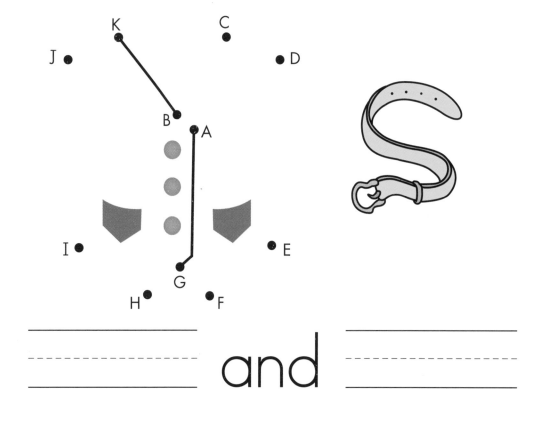

_____ and _____

▶ Trace.

wind

gift

milk

pink

▶ Connect the dots. Color it pink. What is it?

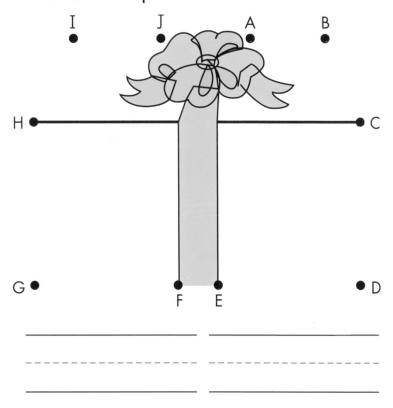

_____   _____

- - - - - - - - - - - - - -   - - - - - - - - - - - - - -

_____   _____

Trace.

j u mp   b u mp

b u lb   b u nk

Connect the dots. What is it?

E

D

C   F

G

H

B

A   I

fun to _____ rope

    EMC 4178 • © Evan-Moor Corp.

▶ Read. Match.

pink mask

milk and a belt

jump in the sand

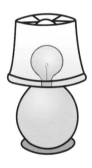

bulb in a lamp

Read. Draw.

sand in the wind

Read. Color.

pink milk

▶ **Read the story.**

I can run in the wind.
I can jump in the sand.
Sand is hot.
Sand is fun!

▶ **Read. Draw.**

Sand is fun!

▶ Trace.

 cake 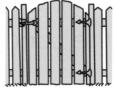 gate

 wave 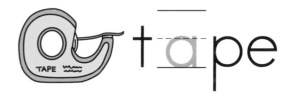 tape

▶ Connect the dots. What is it?

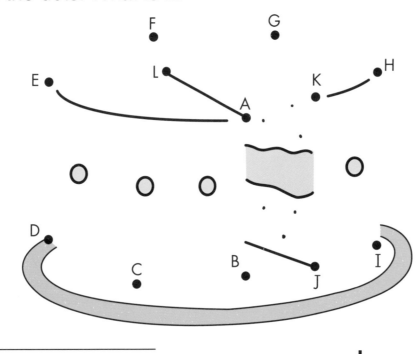

_____
- - - - - - - on a plate

EMC 4178 • © Evan-Moor Corp.

▶ Trace.

 bike 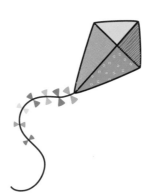 kite

5 five 9 nine

▶ Connect the dots. What is it?

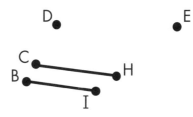

_____ in the wind

▶ Trace.

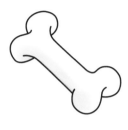 b_o_ne  r_o_pe

 r_o_se  n_o_se

▶ Connect the dots. What is it?

B •   C •

     D •

Q •   A •

P •   E •

R •   F •

O •   I •

N •   H •   G •

J •

M •   K •

L •

dog _____

▶ Trace.

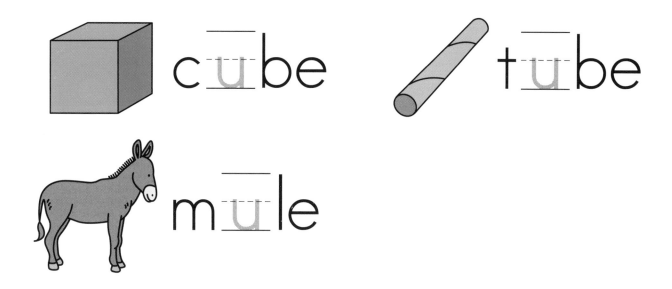

cube   tube

mule

▶ Connect the dots. What is it?

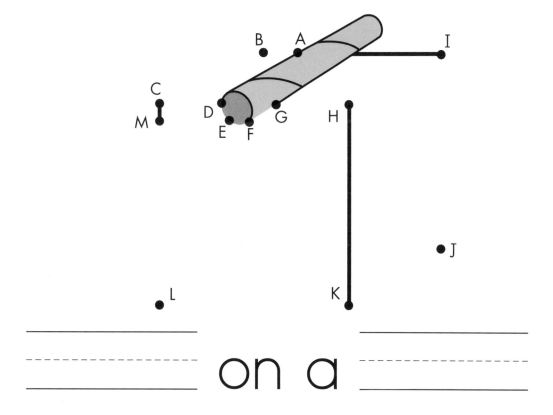

_____   _____

- - - - - - - on a - - - - - - -

_____   _____

Read. Match.

rose on a cake

nine on tape

five on a cube

mule at a gate

EMC 4178 • © Evan-Moor Corp.

▶ **Read the story.**

I got a red bike.
June gave it to me.
I ride my bike home.
I wave to June.

▶ **Read. Draw.**

I can ride a bike.

Trace.

Connect the dots. What is it?

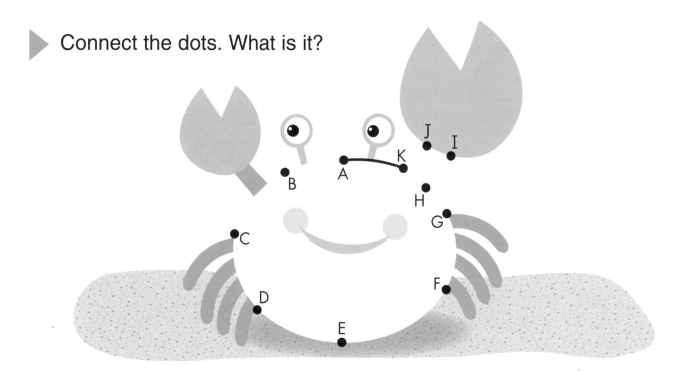

_____
_____ in the sand

▶ Trace.

 sl e d

 st e p

 st e m

▶ Connect the dots. What is it?

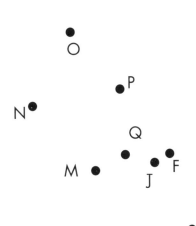

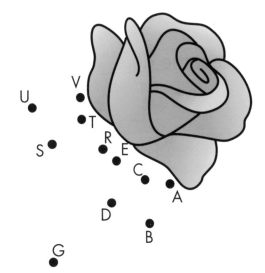

long _____ rose

▶ Trace.

 sw__i__m

 dr__i__p

 cr__i__b

 cl__i__p

▶ Connect the dots. What is it?

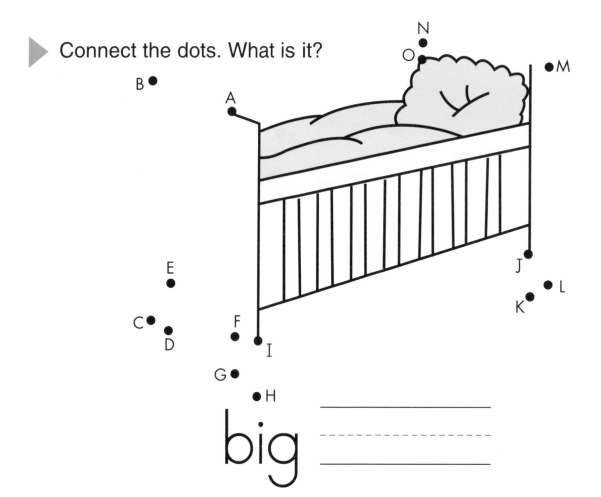

big _____

EMC 4178 • © Evan-Moor Corp.

▶ Trace.

st o p   sp o t

fr o g

▶ Connect the dots. What is it?

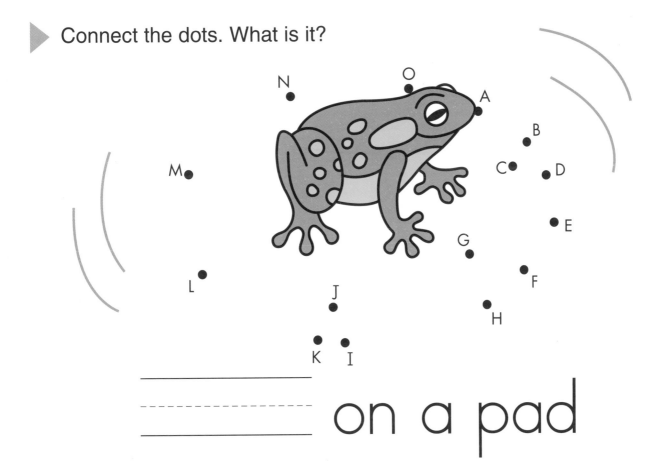

_____ on a pad

▶ Trace.

drum   plum

plug   skunk

▶ Connect the dots. What is it?

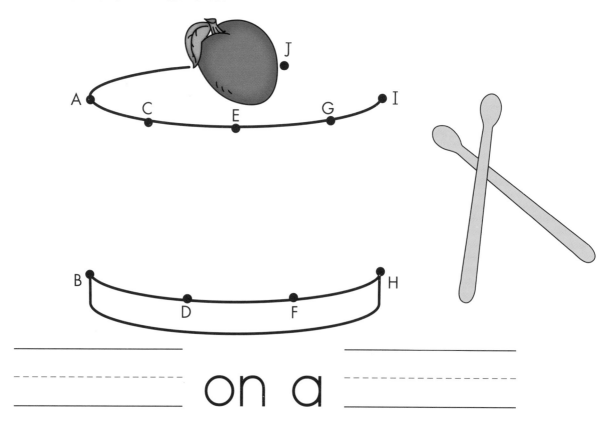

_____   _____

on a _____

    EMC 4178 • © Evan-Moor Corp.

▶ Read. Match.

plum and clip

flag on hat

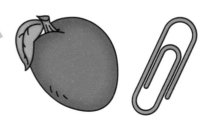

frog on step

clap and snap

▶ **Read the story.**

My pet is a frog.
My frog can hop.
He can hop on a drum.
Tap, tap, tap!

▶ **Read. Draw.**

I can tap a drum.

▶ Read. Match.

dog on a sled

bike at a stop

skunk in a nest

mule in the sun

Read. Draw.

The red bug can jump.

Read. Draw.

I like cake and milk.

EMC 4178 • © Evan-Moor Corp.

▶ Cut and glue to tell what comes next in the story.

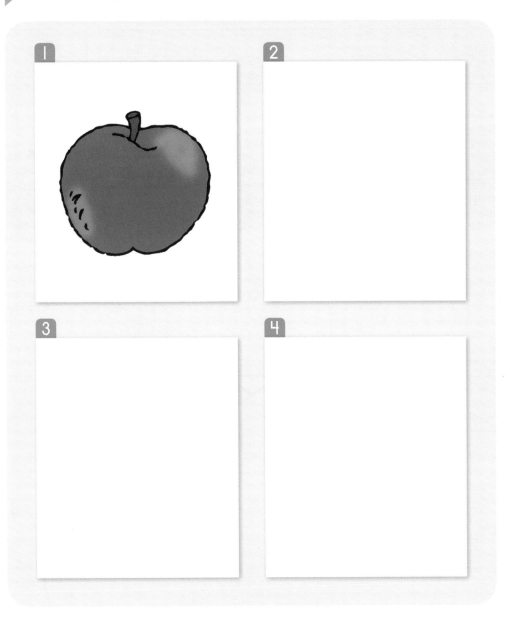

I have a big apple.
I take one bite,
Then two.
How I love apples.
Oh, yes, I do!

Big Apple

▶ Trace the words.

I have an apple.

▶ Finish the picture.
Then color it.

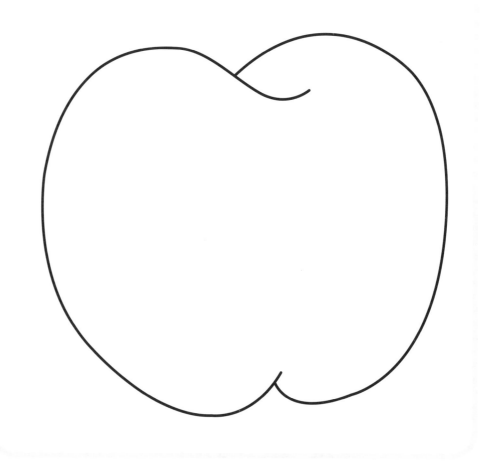

▶ Cut and glue to tell what comes next in the story.

Today is my birthday.
Mom made a cake.
I ate a big slice
And left crumbs on the plate!

Birthday Cake

▶ Trace the words.

I have a cake.

▶ Finish the picture.
Then color it.

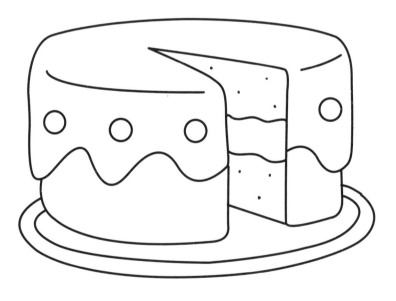

Cut and glue to tell what comes next in the story.

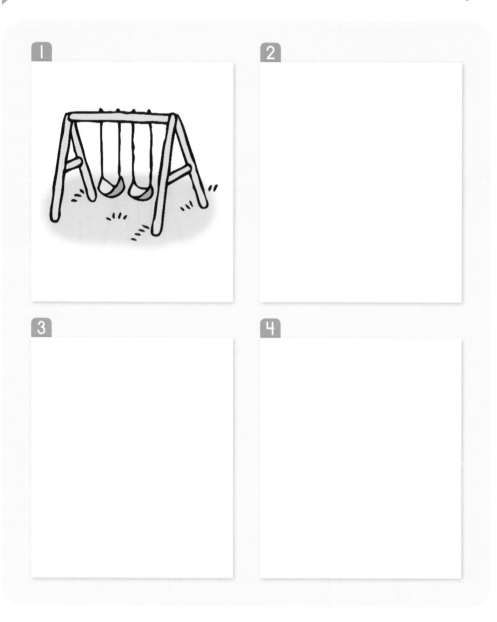

I like the swings,
But I choose the slide.
I go up the ladder
And enjoy the ride!

Day at the Park

▶ Trace the words.

I like to swing.

▶ Finish the picture.
Then color it.

Cut and glue to tell what comes next in the story.

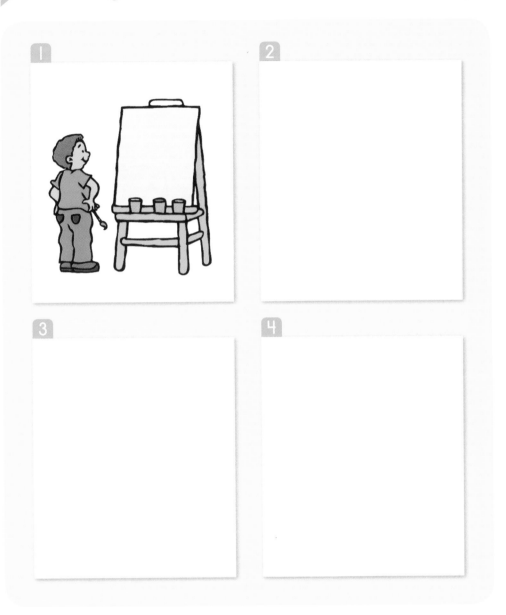

I like to paint.

First there's a tree, and then a sun.

Finally, a house.

Now my picture is done!

Painting

> Trace the words.

I can paint.

> Finish the picture.
> Then color it.

▶ Cut and glue to tell what comes next in the story.

First I'll pick some flowers.
Then I'll ride my bike.
When the day is over,
Then I'll say good night!

▶ Trace the words.

I like my bike.

▶ Finish the picture.
Then color it.

Cut and glue to tell what comes next in the story.

| 1 | 2 |
| 3 | 4 |

I have a ball and Jake has a mitt.
Tom has a bat. It's a sunny day.
Amy comes running and then she says,
"Hey, everybody! Let's play! Let's play!"

▶ Trace the words.

I have a ball.

▶ Finish the picture.
Then color it.

▶ Cut and glue to tell what comes next in the story.

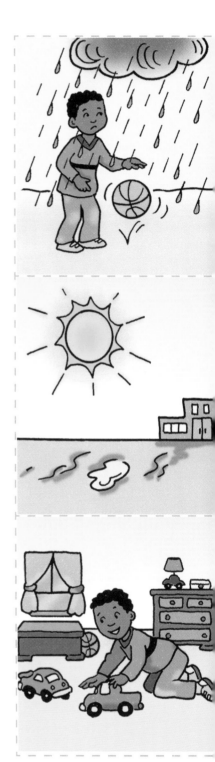

I see a cloud.
Then comes rain.
I go inside to play.
The sun comes out
And dries the rain.
Then I say, "Hooray!"

▶ Trace the words.

I see rain.

▶ Finish the picture.
Then color it.

▶ Cut and glue to tell what comes next in the story.

I had a cold pop
On a hot summer day.
Little by little,
It melted away!

Summer Treat

▶ Trace the words.

▶ Finish the picture.
Then color it.

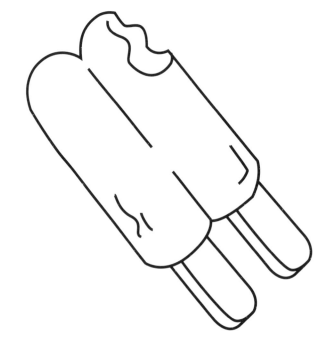

▶ Cut and glue to tell what comes next in the story.

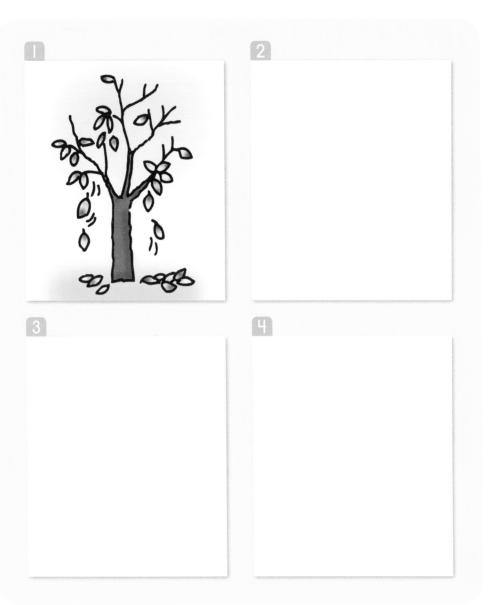

Now it's time to rake the leaves.
We'll make a big soft pile.
When the pile is deep enough,
We will play a while!

Fall Fun

▶ Trace the words.

I see leaves.

▶ Finish the picture.
Then color it.

▶ Cut and glue to tell what comes next in the story.

I look out the window.
That's snow that I see!
I go out, make a snowball,
And soon I have three!

Winter Snow

EMC 4178
© Evan-Moor Corp.

EMC 4178
© Evan-Moor Corp.

EMC 4178
© Evan-Moor Corp.

▶ Trace the words.

I can play.

▶ Finish the picture.
Then color it.

Seasons

▶ Cut and glue to tell what comes next in the story.

In the spring, it is rainy.

In the summer, plants grow.

In the fall, it is windy.

In the winter, it snows.

▶ Trace the words.

I like snow.

▶ Finish the picture.
Then color it.

Cut and glue to tell what comes next in the story.

When I was a baby,
I slept inside a crib.
Every day I'm growing.
Soon I'll be so big!

I Am Growing

▶ Trace the words.

I can grow.

▶ Finish the picture.
Then color it.

▶ Cut and glue to tell what comes next in the story.

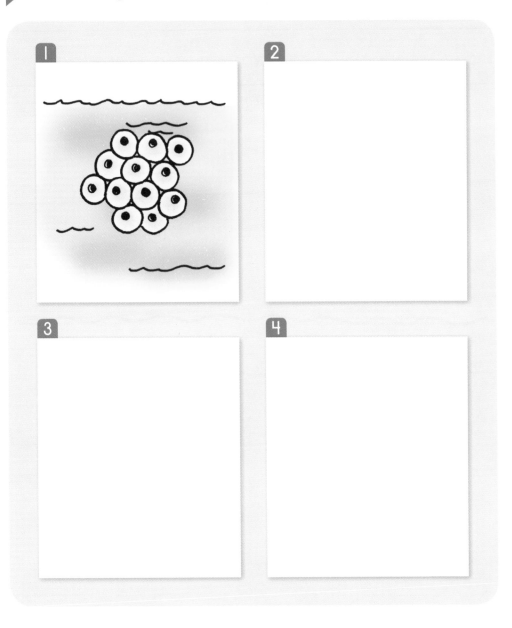

A mama frog lays eggs.
A tiny tadpole comes out.
The tadpole grows and grows
Into a frog that hops about!

A Frog Grows

▶ Trace the words.

I see eggs.

▶ Finish the picture.
Then color it.

Cut and glue to tell what comes next in the story.

A hungry little spider
A sticky web did spin.
A buzzy little fly
Quickly flew right in!

▶ Trace the words.

▶ Finish the picture.
Then color it.

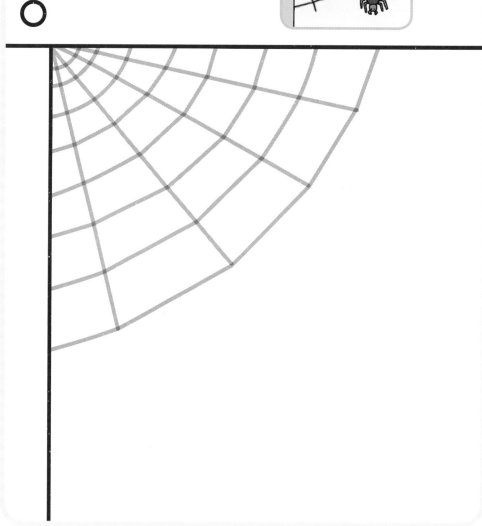

▶ Cut and glue to tell what comes next in the story.

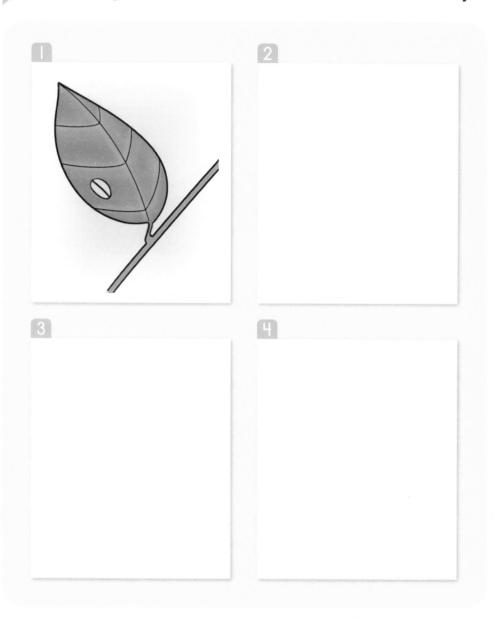

A caterpillar hatches.
It eats a lot. Oh, my!
Then it spins a chrysalis.
Oh, look! A butterfly!

Butterfly

Trace the words.

I see a butterfly.

Finish the picture.
Then color it.

▶ Trace with your finger.

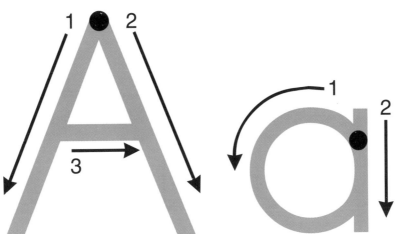

▶ Trace with your pencil.

A A A A

a a a a

ant   ant   ant   ant

Bb

▶ Trace with your finger.

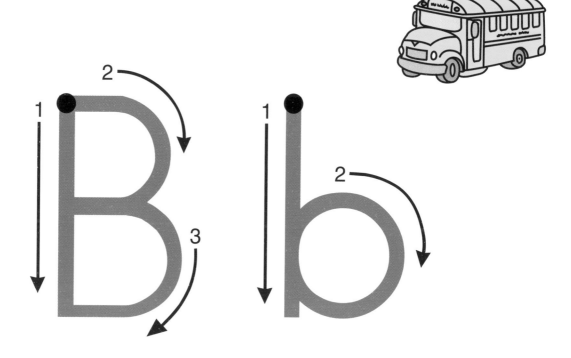

▶ Trace with your pencil.

B B B B

b b b b

bus   bus   bus   bus

▶ Trace with your finger.

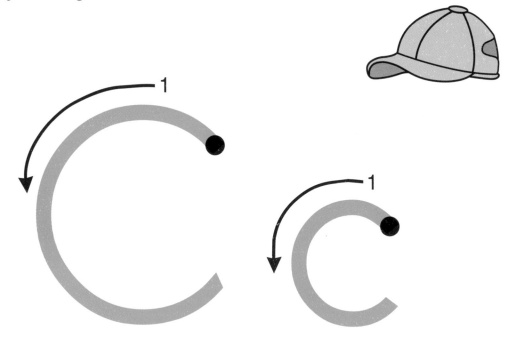

▶ Trace with your pencil.

C C C C

C C C C

cap   cap   cap   cap

Dd

▶ Trace with your finger.

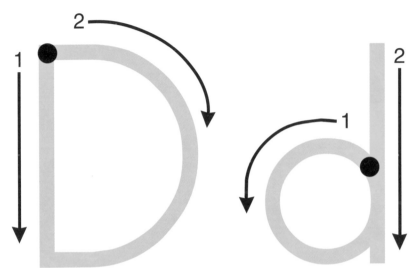

▶ Trace with your pencil.

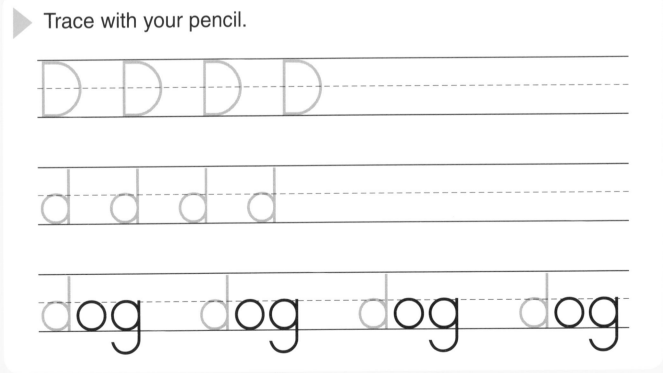

▶ Trace with your finger.

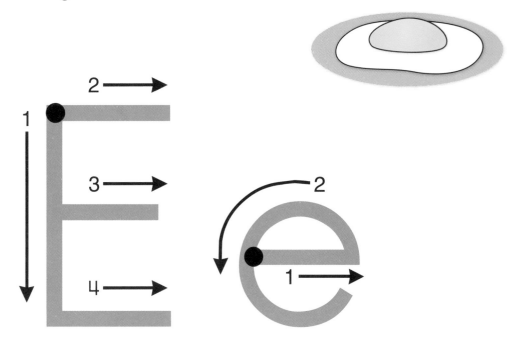

▶ Trace with your pencil.

E E E E

e e e e

egg egg egg egg

Ff

▶ Trace with your finger.

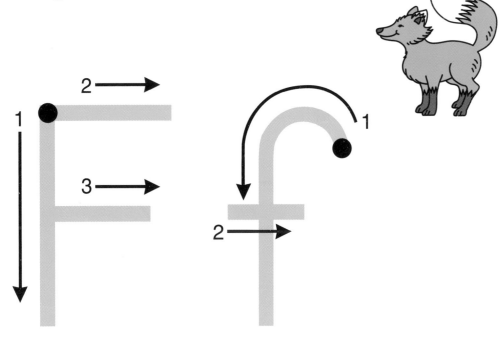

▶ Trace with your pencil.

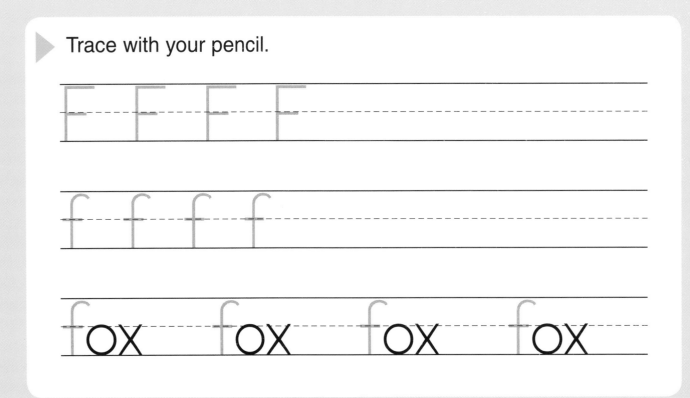

▶ Trace with your finger.

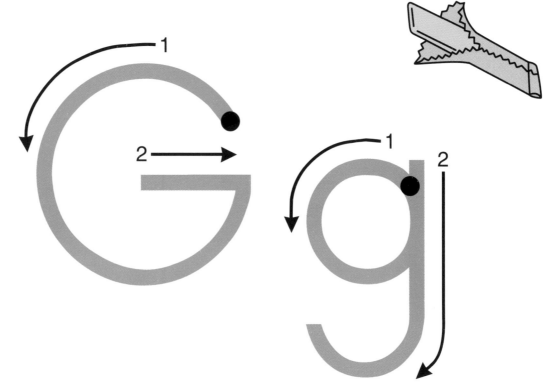

▶ Trace with your pencil.

G G G G

g g g g

gum gum gum gum

Hh

▶ Trace with your finger.

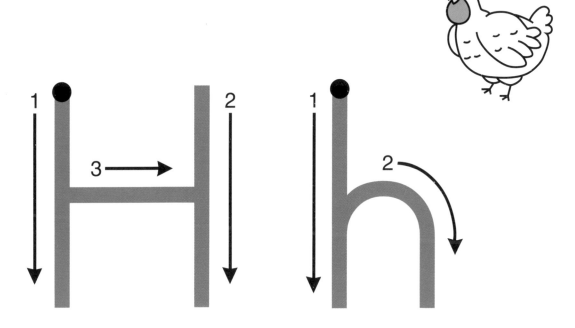

▶ Trace with your pencil.

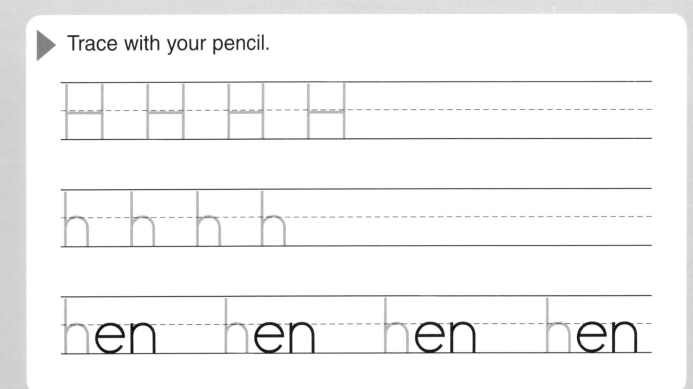

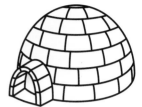

▶ Trace with your finger.

▶ Trace with your pencil.

igloo igloo igloo

J j

▶ Trace with your finger.

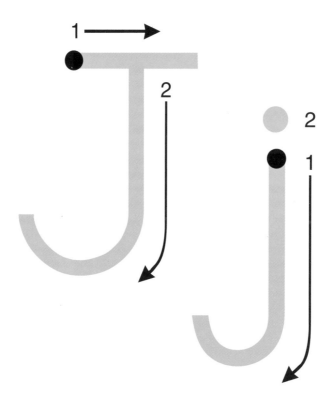

▶ Trace with your pencil.

J J J J

j j j j

jet   jet   jet   jet

▶ Trace with your finger.

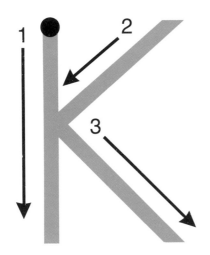

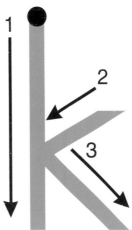

▶ Trace with your pencil.

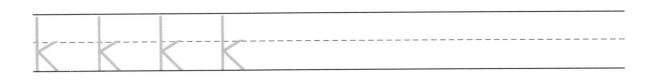

kite   kite   kite   kite

L l

Trace with your finger.

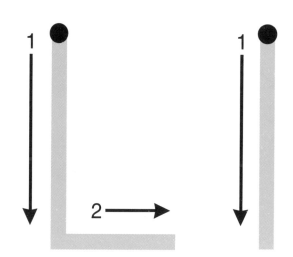

Trace with your pencil.

og og og og

EMC 4178 • © Evan-Moor Corp.

▶ Trace with your finger.

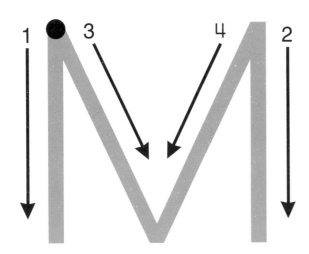

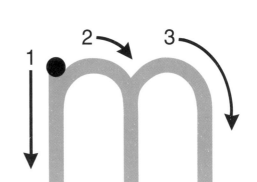

▶ Trace with your pencil.

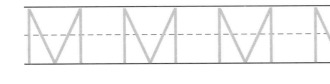

Nn

▶ Trace with your finger.

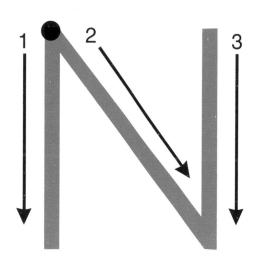

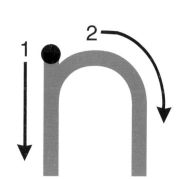

▶ Trace with your pencil.

EMC 4178 • © Evan-Moor Corp.

Trace with your finger.

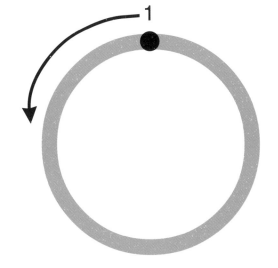

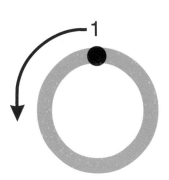

Trace with your pencil.

octopus octopus

Pp

▶ Trace with your finger.

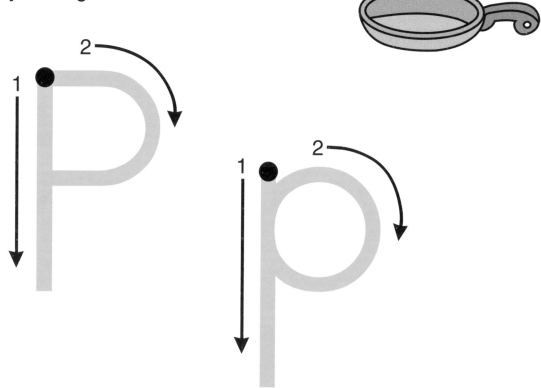

▶ Trace with your pencil.

P P P P

p p p p

pan pan pan pan

Trace with your finger.

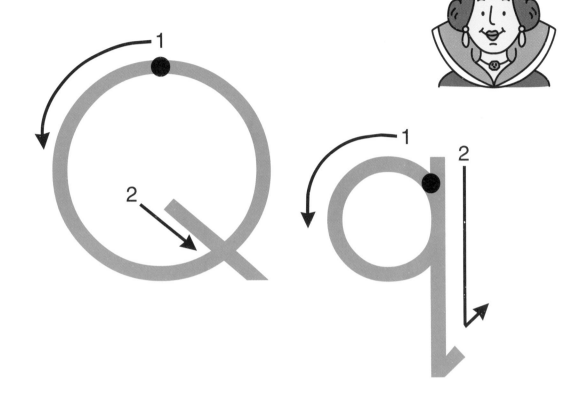

Trace with your pencil.

Q Q Q Q

q q q q

queen queen queen

Rr

Trace with your finger.

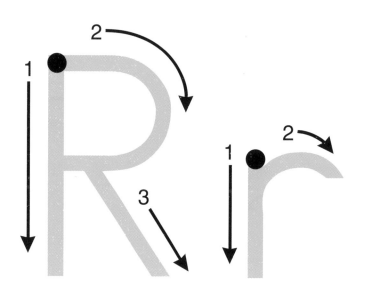

Trace with your pencil.

R R R R

r r r r

red red red red

EMC 4178 • © Evan-Moor Corp.

▶ Trace with your finger.

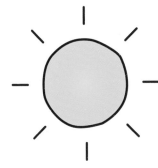

▶ Trace with your pencil.

S   S   S   S

s   s   s   s

sun   sun   sun   sun

T t

EMC 4178 • © Evan-Moor Corp.

▶ Trace with your finger.

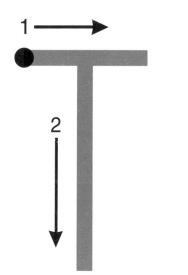

▶ Trace with your pencil.

T T T T

t t t t

ten   ten   ten   ten

▶ Trace with your finger.

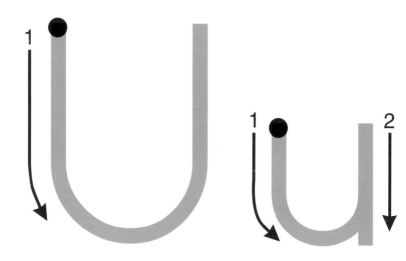

▶ Trace with your pencil.

U U U U

u u u u

up up up up

V v

Trace with your finger.

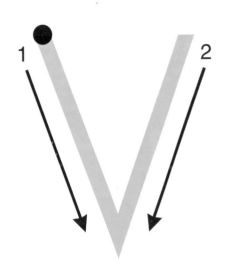

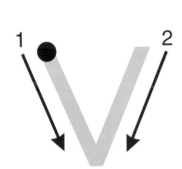

Trace with your pencil.

V V V V

v v v v

van van van van

EMC 4178 • © Evan-Moor Corp.

▶ Trace with your finger.

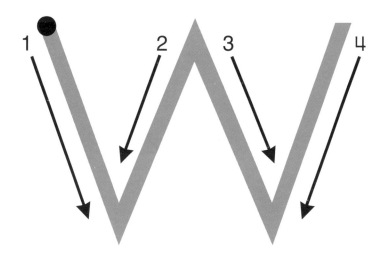

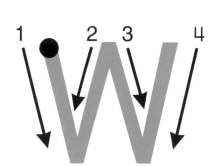

▶ Trace with your pencil.

wig   wig   wig   wig

X x

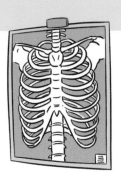

▶ Trace with your finger.

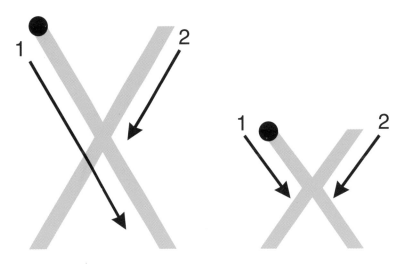

▶ Trace with your pencil.

X X X X

X X X X

X-ray X-ray X-ray

EMC 4178 • © Evan-Moor Corp.

▶ Trace with your finger.

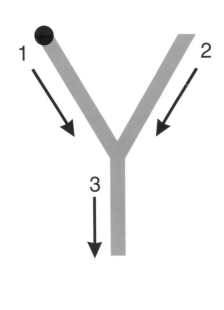

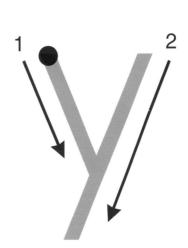

▶ Trace with your pencil.

Y Y Y Y

y y y y

yak   yak   yak   yak

Z z

▶ Trace with your finger.

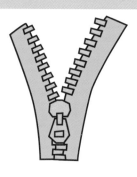

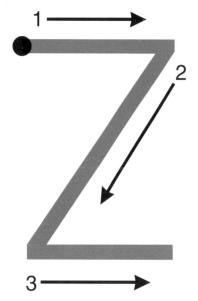

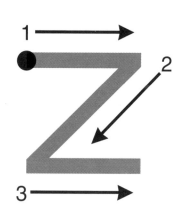

▶ Trace with your pencil.

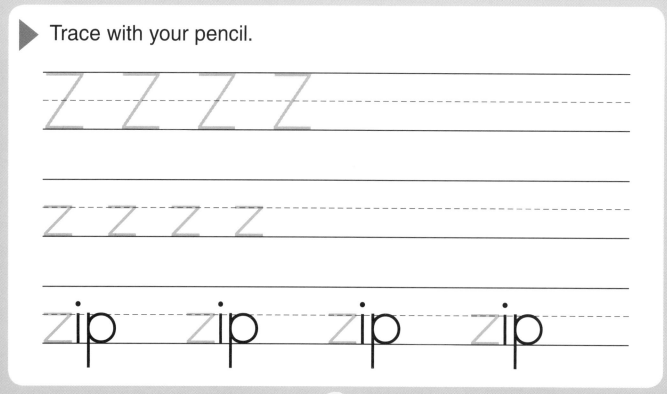

EMC 4178 • © Evan-Moor Corp.

▶ Trace. Write the missing letters.

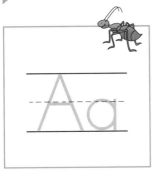
Aa

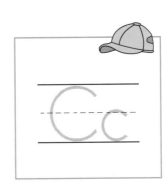
Cc

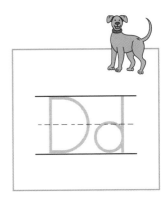
Dd

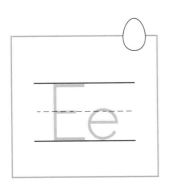
Ee

Ff

Hh

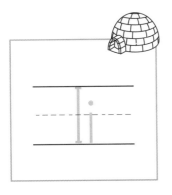
Ii

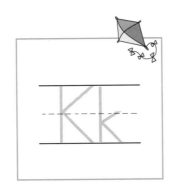
Kk

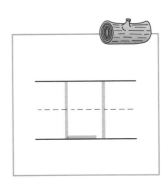
Ll

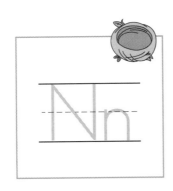
Nn

Oo

Alphabet Review

Write the missing letter.

h m t v

an

en

op

en

Printing Letters

▶ Write the missing letter.

___un

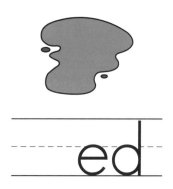

___ed

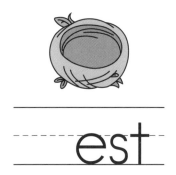

___est

___et

▶ Write the word.

dog   bus   cap   pan

_____

- - - - - - - - - -

_____

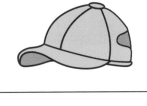

_____

- - - - - - - - - -

_____

_____

- - - - - - - - - -

_____

_____

- - - - - - - - - -

_____

Printing Words

▶ Write the word.

ant   gum   fox   wig

_____
- - - - - - - - - - - - - -
_____

_____
- - - - - - - - - - - - - -
_____

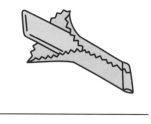

_____
- - - - - - - - - - - - - -
_____

_____
- - - - - - - - - - - - - -
_____

EMC 4178 • © Evan-Moor Corp.

Answer Key

Please take time to go over the work your child has completed. Ask your child to explain what he or she has done. Praise both success and effort. If mistakes have been made, explain what the answer should have been and how to find it. Let your child know that mistakes are a part of learning. The time you spend with your child helps let him or her know you feel learning is important.

Page 2

Page 3
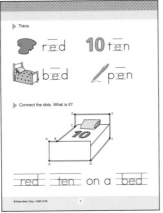

Page 4
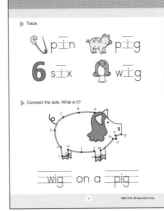

Page 5

Page 6
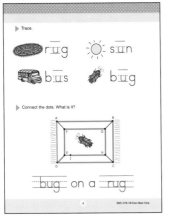

Page 7
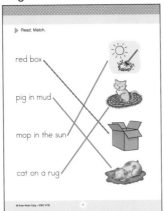

Page 8

Page 9

Page 10
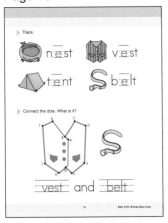

Page 11

Page 12
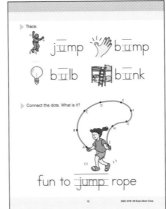

Page 13
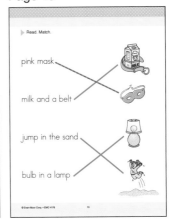

Page 14

Page 15

Page 16

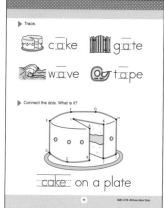

Page 17

Page 18

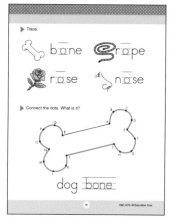

Page 19

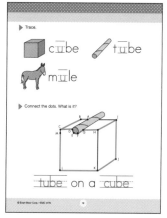

Page 20

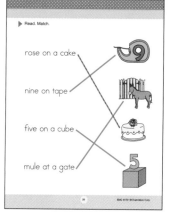

Page 21

Page 22

Page 23

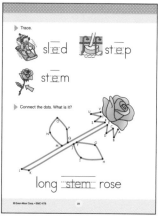

Page 24

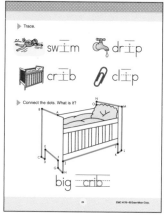

Page 25

EMC 4178 • © Evan-Moor Corp.

Page 26

Trace.

drum   plum
plug   skunk

Connect the dots. What is it?

plum on a drum

Page 27

Read. Match.

plum and clip

flag on hat

frog on step

clap and snap

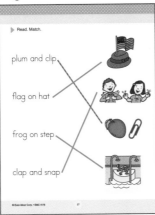

Page 28

Read the story.

My pet is a frog.
My frog can hop.
He can hop on a drum.
Tap, tap, tap!

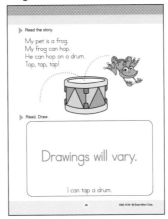

Read. Draw.

Drawings will vary.

I can tap a drum.

Page 29

Read. Match.

dog on a sled

bike at a stop

skunk in a nest

mule in the sun

Page 30

Read. Draw.

Drawings will vary.

The red bug can jump.

Read. Draw.

Drawings will vary.

I like cake and milk.

Page 31

Cut and glue to tell what comes next in the story.

Page 33

Cut and glue to tell what comes next in the story.

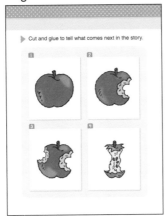

Page 35

Cut and glue to tell what comes next in the story.

Page 37

Cut and glue to tell what comes next in the story.

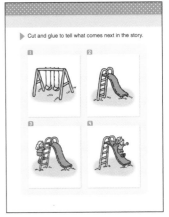

Page 39

Cut and glue to tell what comes next in the story.

Page 41

Cut and glue to tell what comes next in the story.

Page 43

Cut and glue to tell what comes next in the story.

Page 45

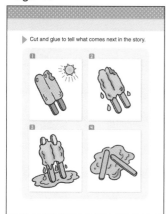

Page 47

Page 49

Page 51

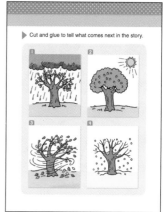

Page 53

Page 55

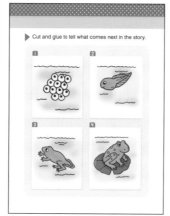

Page 57

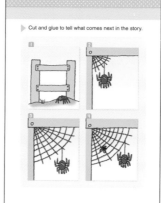

Page 59

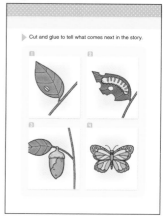

Page 89

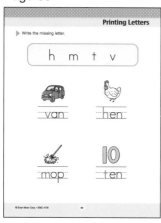

Page 90

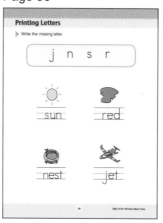

Page 91

Page 92

EMC 4178 • © Evan-Moor Corp.